Unrest

D1518985

Unrest

Joanna Rawson

Graywolf Press

Copyright © 2009 by Joanna Rawson

Publication of this volume is made possible in part by a grant provided by the Minnesota State Arts Board, through an appropriation by the Minnesota State Legislature; a grant from the Wells Fargo Foundation Minnesota; and a grant from the National Endowment for the Arts, which believes that a great nation deserves great art. Significant support has also been provided by the Bush Foundation; Target; the McKnight Foundation; and other generous contributions from foundations, corporations, and individuals. To these organizations and individuals we offer our heartfelt thanks.

Special funding for this title has been provided by the Jerome Foundation.

Published by Graywolf Press
250 Third Avenue North, Suite 600
Minneapolis, Minnesota 55401
All rights reserved.

www.graywolfpress.org

Published in the United States of America

ISBN 978-1-55597-536-4

2 4 6 8 9 7 5 3 1
First Graywolf Printing, 2009

Library of Congress Control Number: 2009926845

Cover design: Jeenee Lee Design

Cover photo: Honeybee hive (Apis mellifera) © PunchStock

For my daughters—

Piper Meriwether Mohring & Cricket Kalliope Mohring

Contents

In the dark times
Will there also be singing?
Yes, there will also be singing
About the dark times.

    (Brecht)

Wind Camp

I can't seduce these raucous birds.

Or sneak up on a willow while they riot there.

Look—even my shadow's a suspect in this dark.

I can't approach without startling from them
an insurgent cursing that gusts and stutters down the trunk.

The weeping limbs ripple in alert as if they've been started by wind
that steals through thistle toward their camp.

I can't manage to net them in my grip.
I can't seem to accomplish any sort of government,

any hold over these unruly crows who nest in rags
and scream at the blowback their quarrelsome cries.

Still, they allow me to stay in the vicinity—

many nights, right here among them, as they activate the dust
and carry on disturbing the perilous air.

Even in their mercy, I believe they understand

my wanting to end their song.

Kill-Box

1.

The air at first smells only of cool steel and chaff.

The air isn't fresh but isn't so old—at a standstill, let's say, a halt
on a spur track there in the train-yard.

The air—and by the air
I mean the cube of breathable space inside the boxcar—

isn't going to be enough.

Meaning the total number of available breaths.

Which you could tally out, divided by the number of stowaways on board,
to figure how much time the 11 of them—

even as the train was picking up speed out of Matamoros, however long ago,
midday, midway into June, snaking its way across the border—

have left. Which isn't enough.

They're inside the grain hopper, the 55 foot long 15 high 100 ton Union Pacific boxcar with
3 compartments and center loading hatch.

Our passengers aren't anybody to speak of.
They're not newsworthy yet.

What matters about them is their illegality—

which on this particular day, under this sun,

having just come to a stop, somewhere in Oklahoma, evening now,
having failed to make their connection, and no one in earshot,

is, at least for them, what keeps all their attention on breathing.

Isn't it getting trickier to keep track of things—air, sense, syntax, the line, etc.?
someone thinks from inside wherever.

Isn't it starting to get a bit hot in here? another thinks from a corner of
the box.

2.

4 women, 7 men.
Paid a *coyote* $1500 each for the ride.
The hatch locked from outside.

This according to the sources who afterward sort out
situations like this—

a border agent, a clerk, reporters on deadline, all of whom file such incidents
in the cumulative keeping track of these kinds of bodies—

these who got up one morning and went about the ordinary business of
smuggling themselves into a boxcar, and crossed.

And that now, among themselves, begin to murmur yes,

yes it does seem to be getting hot.

———————————————

The garden at my place is an old garden somebody else planted.

I've been taking care of it for a while now,
I whack at it and prune the fringes and stake what falls over
in the midsummer heat, but still

it keeps insisting on going almost wild, and arguing's not much use.

Anyone who knows anything about gardens wouldn't call this
a civilized sort of haven.

Whoever designed it—
decades ago, I'm guessing, by the cast of the shadow of the apple tree—
must've had in mind the making of a sanctuary, a place of rest.

I can imagine the gardener studying the microclimate,
taking notes on the global-positioning of the light at set times of day

in order to custom-plant the border that runs the length of the yard.

Still, so many invasives
sprout every spring like mad and run rampant through what's planted.

Ribbon-grass sprints across the walk.
Stonecrop steals into whatever crevice it wants, and the spring poppy crop
riots like a black-eyed full-blaze wildfire.

   3.

It must've been a kind of freedom they figured they were about to
happen into. No matter how it got lost

in translation along the way, in the beginning

it was as if it might occur to them—

getting across, getting free, as if they might almost by chance
encounter it, enter its territory, its state, and, suddenly, in the instant
of demarcation, be ever after able to stay there,

the way any of us giving it enough thought could narrate our own backstories
into a before and an after the fill-in-the-blank event

(the birth, the death, the siren, the call, the lapse, the scouring-out of the mind
through one long night and, then, at the end of it,

the illuminated clearing—).

As if the border were that crease.

As if it might have been a way to alter the itinerary of their fates

that veered off course and into these salt-flats, five hours past 100 degrees,
now that the water's run out,

though right now they're just concerned
with starting to shift, to murmur, to panic and even, a few, freak, and bang,

bang, bang.

4.

About this garden that's disintegrating.
About this dry teasing heat yesterday's accumulating cumulous clouds
meant to fix.

The last iris slaves on.

About this spiral of dust starting to rise into the air like a startled girl's throat.

And these birds that crane their heads into the drought
that just this morning blew the heads off the purple thistles.

About the wind aiming at the fence it means to break its spine on.
About the fence, that won't relent.

5.

About the plume of dust that had risen in their wake
and now settles.

About the proving ground, about the drift of filings, flecks, of splinters and chaff
that litters it and is visible

to no one. About the no one.

There is a wall upon the flat salt earth—
something there is about it that isn't going to let them go,

something about its very nature that isn't going to give us knowledge
of just what it was took place in the souring air it traps.

How long did the banging on it go on?

Exactly what sort of noise did the collateral spray of their one last bang on this hot
communicating wall make?

That no one heard as it rippled out?
Metallic, the odor of a bloodied fist, into the lot—anyone?

Haven't we asked these questions of boxcars?

6.

Right about now the evening sky's ripe
for a mid-season shower of fire off falling stars, flowering fires late in the far-off fields

according to the forecast, which follows the breaking
news that we're living now in a "target-rich environment,"

as it's put by those whose say-so seems to describe the current state of
precariousness as a prediction,

a weather just now coming into being on its way here, worsening,

in this lot ringed by hallowed, fallow wilderness that answers
the passing of trains in the dusk

merely by trembling.

———————————

The gilded larches deliver their knock-down argument in favor of the reckoning
summer-singed light

even as the garden's busy being beautiful
burning.

There's nothing but sinkholes left of the thousand and then some ephemerals that blew open
under the dead leaves, and soon fled at the threat of heat.

Now the garden's stunned, sunstruck at dusk.
Against the bruised skyline lean the hurt stalks.

Rioting aphids over-run the patch of phlox no one's tended in weeks.

There's so much pollen in the air by now it's as if a sepia coats the day,
and the daylilies release their daylong blooms like a sigh let out of the ground.

Turns out most of what goes wrong in a garden

does without meaning to,
without malice, without fault, without meaning.

7.

As soon as the sun goes down, they swarm.
As soon as the map goes black, they come running crawling fleeing.
Come at the border in a drill across the hardpan at it and at it.

The noise of buzzing goes with it.
It's this buzzing the traffic of their bodies kicks up that won't quit.
It works into the inner ear, it sticks and won't, on anyone in earshot, have mercy and quit.

The grit holds the day's heat.

According to their feet the border's a predicament—
this stampede across it, this flushing out into the dark run of the flatland,

this rushing fast of five, six hundred bodies a night out of the makeshift shanty camps

the wind's gusted up against, this dune of ash blown into a bias
as the exodus starts at dusk, all their gazes trained on the sky,

fastened there on the firmament waiting for the light to die.

Around Naco, stadium floods switch on and hit the terrain with hot white fluorescence
the locals call house lights.

Into it *coyotes* send decoys at just past twilight, the opening salvo.

Then the wave hits, quailing in panic over open ground.

Every night it's this script and the next and every next night and whoever's snagged
goes at it all over again the next after that.

In Matamoros, they race at the dark cars and scale up and wedge in and wait for the click of
the latch.

In Tijuana they cram behind dashboards and cross the checkpoints with bruises
the shapes of springs and jacks and knobs blooming in their skins.

In Calexico they float on hitched logs in a reeking green stream that's skinned in trash.

In Nogales there's a tunnel that runs a quarter-mile—when a crosser inside faints
whoever's next crawls in and yanks them back by the ankles and then goes.

One field report calls the stopping of these incursions a basic exercise
in swatting flies.

8.

I come into the garden to kill rampant dill-weed at dusk.
The light says what's been unleashed this season can't be stopped

and whatever might have been on fire still is—sunflowers, asters,
in the downslide of these bat-roiled late twilit hours

when the mind with its static of thought thrums in its want of some rest.

In the stadium across the freeway there's a game on—the players, just kids,
and their fans and a band going at it for all they're worth.

Over here, on this side, each green stalk that's been seized by the day's blazing
hazards the unfurling of its head into the dimming light

that at this time of day seems always at risk
of slipping free of all government and going off into free air.

Pine green, olive green, emerald green, tea green, forest green, sage green, ultra green,
clover green, electric green, panic green

with the ecstatic vibrato of crickets like an undertow,
and then the feel of OK, yes—something approaching a calm.

Then the thought that feeling just about anything (bliss, distress, you name it)
might by now feel like enough.

Then the wanting to be able to come to a rest here and the actual being able to
even farther apart,

with the eschatology of every twilight this sense of being scoured out in the trying.

On the other side of the traffic,
one team scores and triggers wild cheering, a cannon fires, a fight song starts up and
plays itself out

in mid-air, scattering the assembled swallows like scraps of ash across the sky.

The relentless, restless season stumbles across this garden.

The brittle nesting stains green against the acrid soil while this constant wakefulness
wears away the bedding's sheen, and orderliness sunders.

One reason for bothering at all is fireflies,
which defibrillate the wrecked shrubs and rise from the understory
like turbo-candles, in flames.

Another is the wall that's burning,
as if there are rules in play now, here, in the garden, we've never imagined.

What's taken over our place is this fine grit, this pittance of law upon the scorched leaves,
as the dusk-to-dawn floodlights stutter on, spurred by hollow chiming

through the sore weed-stalks

—and then the cheering begins again in the stadium across the way
as fans set off a human wave.

9.

Later, we get talking about how all our talking about all this could go on forever.
Meanwhile, fall's set in

and a train starts up along a track in Oklahoma, and the boxcar in question
picks up speed along with it, in succession,

and comes to a stop finally in Denison, Iowa, in the switching yard there,
in the smallest of blind spots.

It's flatland, it's October, the grain's milled already, it's gone through and used,
what this landscape's good for is already done for and now it's at rest.

Along the tracks, some rough weed—dashing grasses, the goldenrod
that so freely self-seeds.

This is the quiet perilousness that occurs in the air

when it's blown across the fields and into town,
which I know from coming from around here.

What's in the works is a harsh winter again,
you can tell by the way the cut shocks buckle and crack after the hard freeze hits,
and then kneel in the killing frost.

It's not going to go again
with them in it.

It's not clean. It's not dry or ready or empty,
it's just not,

when, on a Sunday, in this late autumn, a worker at the Farm Service Co-op elevator
pries open the sealed hopper brought in after a summer in a storage lot out west
and happens on the remains.

The banging of course stopped.
Way back there, in June.

As the last alternative outcome molted off, and fate turned into
a dizzying, spectacular wind

that's even now, even here, causing the birds to whirl up like soot from these trees.

   10.

A bitten crust.
Fist prints on the wall. Ash.

A shoe.

I come out as the storm starts its blowback operation upon the garden.

Whatever bloomed is shut again, and the wind's climbed
from the hollows to shear whatever's too high for its liking.

The late-blooming hazels are past ripe though the odor they give off seems almost
to keep these hours afloat,

while our light goes about losing the use of its mind

as the air bears such likeness, in this fall wind, to being skinned.

Can't say what's causing what's growing here to list into the squall
just to stand straight

if not sheer will, even as the wind cranks up

and plays what's left of the maple trunk in minor keys turned off-tune
by drought and core rot

years ago someone opened up by punching a fist through the bark,
so that in going about its cadence—

which is all motion and air—all breath—the gusting

snags on the knots and ring-swells enough to cause a sort of haunted canting
to rise from the ruined wood.

This is a tree that should've given in, in surrender,
to its own systematic imperfection.

It should've been removed from the premises
ages ago.

In this garden what's needed to take a thing like this down
isn't weather.

This isn't that kind of garden.

Requiescat

The first day, the cellist played for an hour in the bomb pit.
Whatever audience might have attended had just had their detonated bodies
pitched onto flatbeds.

In rain, in the pit—he played
where they'd been lined up for rations when it blew.

In a minor key he dragged his shadow out kicking the second day,
as if it hated being fastened on.

The third morning it limped unaided to the crater.

Before the sun could explode the ruins into brilliant shards the next,
he improvised a requiem, like a rein on the day.

We're talking now about years into the terror.

It came up anyway against the music.

In the glare in gravel the scorched rubble just this line of notes in the obscene tirelessness of
the dust he kept on for 22 performances on this spot.

After the annihilation, white shock.

After the argument with the shattered light,
as if to oppose utter mortalness itself, he lay down in the heat's siege
sawing at the animal guts of that instrument.

By then no one else could hear it.

There was no one to hear it.

That *it*.

Blowback

Out of nowhere it occurred to me it must be the iris causing this grief.

So all season I've studied the setting-down of inconsolability upon our house
and almost had it chalked up to this cut flower's perfect mercilessness.

But, then, just this morning, I watched its petals and falls
lure the blind-dimmed light into being—
and after awhile couldn't bring myself to associate it with any sadness.

Meanwhile, these other possible reasons inclinate the day:

The neighbor kid's action figures litter the new sod.

My lover goes out to chainsaw the lilacs.

The patina on the doorknob has gone from silver to an ordinary green
from decades of opening and, then, again, closing.

———————————

Somebody handed me this quote as the saddest story ever written:
For sale. Baby shoes. Never worn.

———————————

In 2001 a guy told me this:
My sister sewed me into a bus seat in Tijuana
to get me over the border.

She ripped open the seams of the upholstery
and sat me in position in the bare metal frame
with my arms and head on the rests.

Then she stitched the fabric back up all around me.

It took three days to arrive.

When I ride the bus to work now, I feel like I'm sitting
in the embrace of a ghost.

———————————————

Under the hard scald of the pool's open shower
the bruises on her ribs rise across her skin like a stigmata
the color of plums or barely dawn, as she scrubs
and she hums.

———————————————

In spring, brood rearing starts in earnest in these hives.
If flowers and weather do their part the colonies gain fast.

Young bees in play-flights drift by mistake to the wrong box.
There's no use in denying the disorder.

Later in the season, at clover bloom time, scouting bees come back
with loads of nectar to perform a cure for this anarchy.

The circle they draw is narrow. They run without reversing and tremble.
They're mapping, it's a waltz, it's the bee waggle-dance they do.

In some cases one acts like a lunatic, berserk—I think it's joy.

At night a hive might go into a quiescent state approximating sleep
if the honey flow is for some reason, like invasion, or drought, stopped.

I've seen them form into listless clumps and seem indisposed to flight.
Under these conditions the scout bees get so irked their wings fray.

The others drag them out into the open air and dump the tattered bodies,
still flinching, like winged bombs, into the dirt.

Turns out bees have been pursuing this policy forever.

———————————

We put sheets over the household things to keep them from fading and moths.
The last stair is wiped free of dust. Each shade is one by one drawn.

After a while we sit down on the bare floor with nothing left to be done.

Then we notice—where the rug was, two marks across the floorboards
the cradle made when we dragged it away.

We could go over the checklist again and still everything would be, as it suddenly is,
marred.

———————————

Again he gets up in the blue nocturnal chokehold
and paws through the medicine chest, frantic.

———————————

My own brother says the garden can't bear the administration of this light.

That in such a climate each being already carries its own determined end, its moment.

As though no one is going to live long enough.

As if what needed to be said might never be said.

———————————

I understand that with no warning what was about to happen would be that
the air scraped sideways,

the blast collapsed

like a suddenly very tired voice,

then something in the shock she was in the way of
silvered down, and then the *no* of it—

and then the rest of the blast

on her lashes and the sleeve such a breeze yanked off her dress,
and her stab at half standing

then going down into the wads of hair and lit junk and limbs

into utter red.

——————————————

When the baby was dying
I was certain the night that finally did come would never come.

This night now, when it is only her breathing that keeps
the crickets awake.

——————————————

Three years after we inherited this garden
we figured out how to force the gold apple trees to fruit.

First we shimmed the lateral branches from the leader,
then pinched off all but the prime blooms and hard-cut the green tops.

It being summer, I believe it hurts them now to not grow upward.
Still, in their stunted forms they serve a useful agony in the dirt.

The fruit ripens into prey the storms study.
Chain lightning issues the sour prairie wind that rails at the walls.
It seems like it might be against us, in this gnarled garden,
though for no reason I know.

When the baby sleeps we get up and go out.
Our footsteps reek of dill and rotted castings, and by the last bruised-up light
we notice these apple trees aren't afraid anymore.

For instance, this one doesn't make any motion at all
toward throwing itself upon the mercy of the wind.

Maybe you already know how this ends, but look—

even when the pruned wounds seep
it doesn't kneel,
having committed no wrong, and so having no quarrel with God.

———————————————

Finally we agree to stop talking about the deaths of strangers.

———————————————

Of the bees
I can report it was as if a cathedral hummed.

We stupored the hive with smoke from lit jute.
They ringed our wrists but got too out of it to sting.

Our reach wrecked the wax that was worked from what
the summer clover and early asters translated into, there in the cells.

We knew most of the insects would be dead by spring,

even as our unseasonable hurry in getting the honey out
put their elaborate architecture to ruin.

——————————————

Awhile later another guy told me this:
I was chained to a cinderblock wall for nine years.

First the shackles took away the skin on my ankles and wrists,
then formed cuffs of material that was like bark, which never quit itching.

Later the metal stained these four rings around my numb limbs,
these here, see, the permanent color of bruises.

Even when sleeping I thought about plums,
and, certainly, water.

Highrise

What's going to need to happen here is we just rise from the bed and make it out.

Even as the volume of the ticking spikes.

We're going to have to unplug and exit the house, head for other shelter, an open center somewhere. Otherwise, what?

Either the panic can be sustained or it won't—though just what we're waiting to happen can't quite say.

Could be the wanting of some policy to follow, some strategy, guidelines, rules, as if what we'd thought of as *courage* is up, in these new circumstances, for grabs.

Even if yesterday the word meant something or other.

The soundtrack—live talk, again sirens—sucks and hums enough like singing to hold us still for a moment, while our hoarse breathing twines.

After the fill-in-the-blank of what's occurred (the emergency) when one of us twitches the other's nerves detonate.

What's going to need to happen here, people, is either we let that noise at last lull every ambition to ruin, or we rise up and reach for the keys and get out.

Nightfall now, utterly.

And the debris still thick in the air—isn't it time to?

What'll it take—and where to even go in this predicament about which all this unrest orbits?

Can't say now what it might mean to be law-abiding, we're that far gone.

Every insistence goes into such a thought, this mid-night, mid-season, after which
who knows who'll end up hit by fire or offed in the collateral spray that might, we'll see,
also end up blasting perfume out of the last lilacs grown past wild in the garden.

No good sleep in days and now this, this *this*—
this situation whoever's in charge of

is on the air swearing will never happen again.

As if there were in the matter a say.

As if in the splintering off into unknowingness, right before the power blows, one could
claim to be—what,

undaunted? Free, even?

About which no one has a gut itch of what next to do

—or what this ungovernable wind's about.

Four Seasons Read *The Cloud of Unknowing* to One Landscape

(in spring)

If this is going to be a poem about the weather, then it's bound to also be a poem about poetry—which is, I'm told, either way about holiness.

Like everyone I've tried getting it, holiness I mean, a few times but couldn't—and so, because it's stopped raining out and now the slanted air rhymes this altered light with freight, I'm going to try to follow the instructions in this little book.

Which is hard—be warned! says the author, who's unknown—not unlike how very hard these black nuisance flies work at hatching and rising in this climate.

They're willing but can't do it yet, they don't know the first thing, they're wet, it's humid, and the scribbling they make on the atmosphere won't stick or last.

In this exercise I'd better be lying down, flat out under the swarm stalled in the slick clay where the swelled creek pools in the mossed-up granite pocks of the creek bank.

It's an ill-lit spot where the rotting starts and spreads, the sort of place where our author recommends we kick off a pursuit of what's called here "ecstatic devotion" (note to self: is there another kind?).

Anyway, it says that to get capable of this ecstatic devotion your whole life now must be one of longing.

That you should work away at it until you have this longing.

Also that there is a cloud, it's made of forgetting.

It's actually a whole firmament made of this forgetting, between us and what we're after, call it bliss, union—OK, no evasion: the divine.

It goes on to advise that after you get maybe even an inkling of this longing, try to see if you can get some sort of feeling that might be described as a "moving."

Or no, not movement, what could more reasonably be called a "changing"—suddenly.

It says here it's better to reach out blind, to go at the draft flailing for some kind of dew in the air.

If it goes well, then look: in a sudden: in this understory, the glazed limbs of each tree hang laden with the knuckles of shut silvered petals the gnats mob.

They seem to be ferocious in their work.

   (in summer)

Even so, more thunder hums.

Across the creek air-moss tendrils into the heat and it's just dusk.

It's in this sort of atmosphere the pulse mimics crickets, until the chain-lightning stops their circulation of iambic song here in this crook of quartz-fraught rocks.

I'm afraid I'd really have to know something about what's called in these pages "the soul" in order to undertake this little expedition (but no, it tells us, you don't, and no, there's no other kind).

Even so from here, where the world's gone almost to rumor at twilight, I can still make out the snack wrappers, the spit seeds and shot rafts and casings that litter the far banks, where we've been living.

And still hear the rats at the roots of the wild beets in the ditch, and the soft crushing of box turtles on the warm tar in far-off traffic, and once night hits the dull uncomplicated motors of the crop-dusters swinging up into the moon's blind spot.

Forget all this.

Devote yourself to this forgetting, it says, and then forget that too.

Verse yourself in this forgetting.

It's enough that you should feel moved by you know not what.

Enough that a blundering, earthly stirring occurs in untutored ways.

Give no attention to the ivy clawing at the white scat in the spackled mortar and give no attention to the fireflies like galaxy dust and the burnt sedge and the creek's reeking and none to the willow after a week of heat taking its hair the rest of the way down.

Ferment in this deliberate ignorance, make it your substance, your gist.

In this stupid desire we're told to do this: pick one word—something like "bless" or "bough" or "love," though I'm going straight at the matter with "help"—whatever, it's prayer, so use it to hammer away at the cloud.

Beat away at the cloud, this intervening, high, and terrible cloud, with your sharp little word.

Try to penetrate that darkness that's been always above you with this uttered blurt.

Don't stop, even at daybreak, when the heads of the daylilies steep open.

   (in autumn)

Monstrous beige miscanthus canopies our vantage.

Bats irk the sky that's slung with wisps of thistle the first freeze ripped.

The shocked oak-spurs creak on the banks against the breeze's usual restlessness, or is it recklessness?

Which is a difference only in poems, in which I understand that any distance between words is inconsolable.

Anyway, even, and maybe especially, without my attention the overripe asters emit their fragrance (an invasion so hard to ignore, given its nauseating too-muchness) against the low-slung loess bluffs I'm right now clawing away at in this work.

This sore, abraded terrain delivered into frost.

Vexed—this morning freakishly so.

During which all the material I am, the whole quark and grist corporation, irritates just by being.

Who knows what to do about this ceaseless hot static everywhere?

The book forecasts just such a predicament when it says we're supposed to loathe and tire of all that goes on.

That the time will come when the soul will feel all of its ordinary prayer to have faltered utterly, and will be bewildered.

At this time there is bound to be agony on the part of the soul, which wants nothing but God, but can only feel desolation and dismay.

That this fatigue is a readiness, it's a deep sorrow of spirit like a worn rut in the earth.

It says get to a place where you don't even want to come away from this harrowing occupation, get to where even angels couldn't comfort you.

Frantic, frightened by this weight.

A plight.

And so, because it's stopped meaning out and now the cantled prairie is rimed with the likeness of faltering light, this genuine sorrow is full of holy longing.

Therefore, the delirious carp drive violently into the debris of sunk weeds.

Sour-grained, the ruined willow roots turn slick in the mire of shed skins, under the ice-skinned marsh sealed up in swollen croaking.

(in winter)

It says whoever you might be who possesses this book, don't mention it to anyone unwilling to likewise set out into this curious little expeditionary venturing into nothing and nowhere.

Come here: the air hovers at zero.

Breathing's uneasy, as if the season's last killed blossom had lodged in my chest.

In spite of the influential wind, ice that splints the brittle crippled stalks of the brushfire shatters in flames, even as these clouds keep coming down snow.

Against all reason the worn dirt rut—the *via negativa* that's scrawled down the blown slope—spells this: what we're after, what this longing's been so long for, isn't to be known.

What's wanted is not unlike an ungoverned and snow-blind upsurge of love.

(Don't forget: forget.)

It's against this breaking down, this erasure, the cold burnt air's seized up.

It makes a realm of ephemeral sustenance around us like these wasps' nests strung under the sandstone bluff and still ripening in the white winter sun.

At last, in the bare tree—songbirds, that earlier the leaves obscured.

And it lasts, in the fallow air—this source of the singing, bearing its ecstatic devotion into the atmosphere above the oblivious snow.

All their beings work at it with urgency, though we're cautioned in the last passage that this urge might not endure.

That in time we might find ourselves wanting to once again go toward unsheltered ground, toward a more perilous place than this—

because who could live with any purpose here?

Here in this unburdened, this perfect situation. That is final. That is ever. That is of no earth I know—

The Mark

A black mutt stands on the axis of this earth
which happens, today, to run through this meadow.

This animal, this ridiculous beaten-down thing, doesn't rise, doesn't run,
doesn't spin in the midday glare that takes the last wind
from the wash on the line.

This is a wind that just yesterday stirred a ditch stuffed full of kids
into one wide smear in the matted rush-grass.

Today they're burnt, they're naked except for the capes of squash leaves
blown over them.

Their green sheets reek in the rank sun.

Their skins are riddled with mold.

Bringing us again to the dog, which is marking its stuck place with an x of piss
soured by the rotted entrails it's rolled in.

A gnarled globe of some vegetable lies in the grass, heavier than several of these
human bodies, and not as easy to break open.

It's past usefulness—all the taste's grown out of a thing this size
that should've been picked, that was let go into such swollen monstrousness,

as has this stagnant dog, its genocidal flies, and the gas rising now off the swamp.

Doorway, with Citizen

Balanced in the jamb she doesn't look back into the room or on into the next
but stalls, here, in-between.

She studies the grain of the wood. Notes its flaws.

The behind is closed, the ahead is not yet opened—
at this moment, just a short while into the fray, she's free of any consequence.

Of course it's summer.

Of her stalled self she's made an encampment between before and after,
in a sort of wilderness, where bodily functions stop their fast-forward,
including any terror.

The quick undertow that's fueled this rushing
stills, and all of what she ever loved (bees, lullabies, the rest)
erases from the current tense.

Leaning into the frame, it appears she's entered some sort of caesura
in the riot of appointments and lists.

Not a thing to do here but come to an idle
and wait for a signal to move on.

Oh. It might be the first surrender occurring in her—
the talking on the other side of the threshold, beyond this clearing,
is still too low to make out meaning,

though the voices there seem, suddenly, contentious enough in their cadence

to suggest the start of the argument about her government, her fate
in the thin air ahead.

A Summer under Occupation Reports Its News & Weather

Wash dries on the line three days now.
The air's shot through with dust so wind-slung it sweeps the weeping trees.

It hovers at our chests and at night nearly shrouds the ground.
Fireflies don't quit blinking inside the haze.

There on a white rag the mushrooms are scattered to cure but can't.
Cotton underthings flicker on the wire. Again they're streaked
by blown gold pollen that spots scattershot in the grain.

The kids fall down into the stark grass and count to ten.
Someone's it, on base by the gas tanks.

When they rise, their silhouettes mat the thatch
that stays a shade cooler when they run for cover.

If the game keeps getting played past dark
the outlines of their heavenly bodies will whiten in relief
like the chalk-marks drawn around the shot down.

Wouldn't you know by then the stars will be nearly out.

Some same bird that every evening sings like it's stuck or stung
will come, its sound all over again and back off the bluffs

and make us—floating, up here,

above the dust, on the porch with our dirty gins,
the work done, the lists in our heads shut off—

scream,
like the kids do,

for the same reason.

———————————

Next morning the test pilots go at it again.
Just over the slope from here—they've marked the kill-box for morning runs.

Coordinates, conditions, a season of unrest—
call the war the weather we've been having, almost a climate.

The strafing goes utterly on like strikes against the wind itself.
The first stubborn sunflowers are loaded with blown sand
so even the analogies now are occupied.

Whatever ordnance it is that's intervening in this day echoes its nature
and upon reflection sounds suddenly wildly musical.

We check the kids and every so often the horizon for our bearings,
as if still free,

and stake the hollyhocks, whose spines the slightest tremor tends to
snap.

———————————

Our girl glows against the tobacco shadows.
Fat elderberries stain the truck hood in streaks.

Dark birds hit the hardpan road ruts
and even according to this ill-lit dusk, it's mocking
the sky-stranded rain's doing to this fine dust.

Between it and these shadows her skin's ideal,
an argument for at least a bit of redemption,

not worn, not marred, not party to the sort of mind that could dream up
the war we're at—

no, it's made of opulent heat,
a toddling courseway of audacious occurrence
in the midst of this season's grunt sweat.

All the old growth has been felled across the field.

Among what's left, the drought-addled jack pine thinks ahead about fire.

Its bark's mostly already gnawed off, its such sorry roots
hardly fasten the thing down to this bombing flat
that's dusted in the wake of the morning practice runs.

At times like this, during the dry mean spells that happen here,

the old targets, like the trace of healed-over sores, still rise up
out of the ground, faint, and rapacious.

———————————

The clouds swell with floating rain, and in the gold suffuse
early crickets undertake their first, inconsequential attempts.

No downfall in twelve days and in this heat that's killing.

Dust lifts from the ditches in the least breeze.
What's under it is just hardpan and the clay silt that's turned to brick.

Even if it could pray for otherwise, the ground's not able
to take in rain should the sky decide to.

Under the pine canopy the faint mist that's made it out of the earth
that far dries. The river's so low now.

Willow roots you couldn't tell before were there surface
as the surface drops, and the geodes rise as fists.

The lazy bees in want of sustenance dive and drive along the banks.

In spite of it all the girl leans on an evergreen trunk.
It's older than her, sturdier, with wider girth, so screens her from this porch.

Its bark is all her skin's not—a half-century's worth of wear.
Together they make a column that thrusts and cores this glare from the ground up.

Maybe I should tell you about the injury to it some years ago
(truck backed up, blind spot) or that the scar down its torso

leaks on hot days in spring, as things thaw and start to swell and stick and then
scabs with resin against dry spells like this.

She picks at it absently now—or with intent, can't tell,
no matter what she knows about longstanding hurt.

You can smell the sore once it's opened—
beyond green, and already sealing over from the inside
against yet another attack such as ours.

———————————

Here's where the horse has fallen.
Down among the brittle leaves and first ripe squash.

Nothing's gotten to it yet, though soon the crows.

The girls come to have a look.
The two of them want to lie down beside her hardening flank and do.

The little one runs her entire arms over the animal's side,
down over the washboard ribs where the last breath got out.

The older drowses in the inconsolable grass by her white pet.
She curves her own body to fit the curve of the mare's—

shoulder, spine, rump, and is just as equal as a rider, right now,
could be to grief,

which in a kid at this age is mostly grim, practical work.

People who do it for a living
will take the horse away tomorrow, in a truck.

We're getting things ready. Nothing will be a surprise,
even afterward, after the lift and disposal and the mist that sets in.

The proving ground where this body went down is already marked
by matted thatch, and scorch.

———————————

The girls blow bubbles out over the porch rail.
No breeze means the globes don't float or sink but stick to this scene
backed by limp branches and the gnarled clay banks.

The game's been going on long enough so the porch chairs,
the silly ragged geraniums, one girl's fat doll are all coated in soap
and prism the light across every surface in splatters and smears

while the grown-ups on the other side of the screen
crank up their voices in the heat.

Yesterday wind, today none, maybe it's that, that
and an air temp that turns the solution so viscous, so impossible,
that alters their operation, and wrecks the hang of it they'd gotten.

The big one's just wet herself but no one cares or keeps track here,
we're otherwise occupied, the creek is close and cool

and pretty soon she'll go jump in and rinse and come up spectral in the glare
against the damp shadow of the old trunks.

Clethras and wild ox-eyes are in bloom, rioting at the edge of the yard,
so full of perfume the place has an extra dimension.

It's still too soon for the crickets to quit.
Ivy's obliterating the cyclone fence put in to keep the place safe,

and then the breeze brings along the single siren
that might mean storm.

———————————————

Her hair's strewn in the bedding like willow whips.
The rash on her belly is woven ivy,
which by morning should wilt and die if our girl's fever breaks.

Here's how our panic reconciles:
it's always summer and for a moment the bombing trials stop

and the next, it's these tremors again
here at the edge of the meadow
where a precise shade of ungodly gold sunlight rules.

My neighbor says to not worry, that missing is not, as he puts it, an option.
He's been making some of the runs, some of the mock hits before shipping out.

On his last tour, the kill-box he worked
was at the south-most tip of the desert, and floated like a tease in the heat.

Orders were to take out anything that moved at night. He never saw much
but took it out anyway.

So he says. And says he'd like nothing more
than waking up into this kind of light, as if it were his duty,
until he goes blind.

———————————

When the little one's screaming after every last trick won't quit
I swaddle her deliriously ill body in a sheet and walk

still crazed by no sleep
down through the burned weedfields to the pines.

It's been since this time last year.
No one's cut them again, after what happened
when the move to open the grove up, let some light in,

turned into a cruel pruning
even a week of freak summer storms couldn't do.

When trees like these get indiscriminately thinned with dull tools like that
they seep from the sores.

These never did stop.

The amber sap caught all sorts of spores and gnats
as it ran down the hacked trunks into pools.

The ooze smelled at first almost fresh, vivid,
then went rancid, with an edge like sour iron.

Now the gnarled, unhealed trees
bear likeness to the arthritic limbs you see on old field hands.

We lean against the scarred bark. The child's knocked out from the walk
and the sudden shock of bitter air.

Her fever makes each breath a hot streak it hurts to hear.

Cobwebs mesh the crooks. No birds come.

_____

The drills started up even before daybreak.
The last of the windstorm was just dying back

and the blown willow whips that yesterday littered the river
had flown and stuck to the screens.

The gowns on the line have dried. They're riddled through
with rust-shot, as if the draft had used them for weeping.

The pocks are the orange that happens when air works on blood.

Whatever's getting blown to smithereens over the ridge
is made of metal, whose bored-through odor reeks like the kind of rain
we keep waiting for.

Every effort is made precise by experimental instruments
is what the informational flier tacked to the door this morning spells out.

When the weather turns out wrong, the helianthus and early asters
bloom crooked, like an afterthought to reason.

Its been ages since the leaves have blown in swarms according to natural drafts,
instead of these deadly we dream up.

_____

The engine's noise could be crickets, if you tried hard.

Say it's OK to just go about things on a day like this:
eventually the river goes right through everyone's head,
like a silver cleave.

The Russian sage that draws the shadowline a fence once cast
is turning the wiry panicled purple it does in August,

the kind of sight that tells you to lie the hell down and breathe.

My oldest friend, who'll be 87 this fall, if she remembers things right,
makes a steady racket of crack and pitch with what she's shelling on the porch.

Her hands can't move much since arthritis shocked them
into half-bloomed fists a decade ago, but she's found a way
to do this work.

Can't hear much. Can't see much now at dusk.

Even so she tracks the girl who hangs naked from the porch rail,
over the south sunstruck dill bed.

The blood's gone all to the kid's head. It'll be hours before she says a thing.

The old one's marking the young's every twitch half-blind,
thinking hell, hang there, why not, just strip down and get some air,

dangle over the weeds, maybe drop, do it, do it again and
again and forget there's any anything else to do or be,

one last time before it's time

for someone to start the car, and her to get up
and go down and climb in back and wave and make the slow drive over.

The attendants are waiting, it's all a go.

Someone will bring up your things.

Here's your window. Here's the remote.

The set. The switch.

———————————

When the explosions hit, the kids woke up with a start
into a dark smarting with fire,

and then the drill ripped out there and again and an echo,
or a return round, scattershot, just wild

gunning at whatever fled across the dirt.

When the sorties keep on, we squat down below the sill.

It turns out there are chemicals the brain can let loose in sleep
that paralyze one's body, sometimes for hours.

All that's not automatic quits.
You can't flinch on purpose. Can't turn and can't rise.

It seems you're not even able to defend yourself.

Anything could fly in at these times, and even if lethal
you couldn't.

———————————

Wind snags on the brittle shaft-grass downhill.
A ways off a chainsaw hacks at a payload of wings.

Swallows rise out of the noise and hover in swirls, waiting.
The orchards are parched, their serrated pungency is so long gone.

Even without faith I'm keeping track of the two of them, father and girl—
walking up ahead while the war goes on.

We came to this place to ask for some alteration of ourselves,
for whatever grace might, if any, please, even if we don't even believe,
still, might be had

to cure this child's very small, ill body, and give us this day,

this day our daily war goes on and
on as our shadows cross and trip and kneel in the meadow the sunlight
makes a bed for our exhaustion that also goes on.

Will she be fixed?
—Don't know.

Is there any instrument that could be used?
Any procedure upon her body?
—Again, don't.

Meanwhile, the sheep up the rough slope eat themselves silly on feverweed
in the late heat where just this morning trees made of themselves a provisional shield,

where up higher, I'd say even up on high,
she whose every breath is in our hands presses hard into her father's chest
as he walks on into the sky,

past the hacked-up dry limbs (piles, centuries of them) stacked
in the clearing for burning.

Again the clouds give off another gorgeous twilight, when what's needed is rain.

———————————

Here the dogs lie belly up in the shattered reedstalks.
The small bodies stretch out on dirty rag-rugs, singed in dust.

For this morning's runs the kill-box is small, doable.
Nothing exactly quivers but the quick raids give the air a loose fit.

The kids' skins have been bronzed by days of glorious late glare.

The river's so distilled by now it's turned their hair green.
The air hasn't had a wind in it in days.

All of this, all of everything, is necessary, said someone.

When the five-jet formation dips to its target and rips up the pine slope

the register the day's pitched in
alters so slightly the girls twitch and the animal's fur
twitches and flicks,

and the black cellular flies mobbing their dozing bodies
lift, swarm, and light again, precisely like

the determined machines they are.

_____

We were an hour at the river when the littlest one went missing.
Who last saw her said on the tire-swing. Said screaming
out over the broken clay bank and back naked.

Not a minute ago. Then—

the way a kid can be at your heels
then just gone.

The current and birdsong and talk and all breathing
quit.

Then no, no she didn't. No she wouldn't. No, and
check the road. Check the low
scrub patch she liked, go, somebody, now,
check the rotted-out roots where the black gnats breed,
the silt pool, the slope,

she could be, could've gone, been taken away even if not a minute ago
was right here alive and then,

and then—then out of what

sounds like

nowhere, the next

jet run fires off the bluffs, and
the blowback

bears a *here,* she's down

here, in a rut
in the creek, face up, in the smoke, still,

yes, alive, she's buried

her legs, it's for fun, she's done it for fun, to the knees
so they're stumps,

she's down in the cool mud splayed, playing like she's struck,

like the shot last night on the news she caught

of the dirty-bombed kid
blown into the silt, limbless, shorn
of extremities, and the sickening

gnats in swarm over the sores,

and her gaze trained on our gaze upon her,

as if she wants to see what we must see

as we squat to lift her up.

———————————

In the clearing, in the leaf-cover break, in what's left of the brush ash,
where the horse died down, in the evening

around the mown grass piles in the field,
in costumes cut from bags and charred bark,

the kids rip around barefoot playing who knows what in the bruised air.

Their get-ups are cockeyed, cut crooked and stitched
so even the littlest among us can't see out right.

The crickets are almost over. Their noise did the trick.

The hillside across the river's shot into flame,
strafed by this drought that's made the colors
wilder, quicker.

———————————

Her neck's a twig. Her chin's stuck out in a rough jut,
though the photographer's told her to do just this
in order to snap it.

She's just three, though by the look of her bones runs small.

The shot is shoulders up, just the checkered fringe of dress showing.
No smile, ears out, sun-gold hair shorn, a home job.

Why it's been taken is her right eye.
The thing's swollen nearly shut, and maybe was all the way when she woke.
The lashes sealed it with seeping that dried.

Some kind of stye maybe, or more likely, since it's still summer, a sting.

Not a blow, since there aren't other marks.

A wasp, say, one that got in fast on the wind.
The way they can get under the lid and strike and worsen when you wipe or keep at it
from the itch—anyway she's damaged.

It can't be permanent since no parent would take that.

It's been done in passing, quick, while the eye's still swelled,
a kind of documentation while pollen blows by.

The kid's on her way to somewhere else, she's not maimed, it's not forever or tragic,
just a collision with some miniscule freak thing that had effect,
so it's safe to keep this

photo of a child evidently not disfigured by the strafe of another bomb,

like so many of the others, one who'll go back to being almost
like before.

———————————

Someone's belting the anthem through a bullhorn by the river.
Earlier the same got done with morning hymns.

There's no end in sight to this drought-stupored stretch—

you can tell by the haze rising up off the bluestem like it does right about now
and the way the moths stay low in the slowed, stuck air.

Already the girls laze on the porch cot in their dance things and panties.
No one's brushed their hair for days.

They've hosed down in mist to cure their skin of smoke
but wear crescents of filth in their nails.

All the book covers are curled and the flag furls, the clouds boil.

A pattern of blown glorious roses, the kind you can't get anymore,
has been burned by dull sun onto the floorboards.

The linens are stained sepia by our restless bodies being on them so long.
No one's asleep but there's not much difference.

It could be a kind of celebration—
this being too worn out for more work, with the war amplifying its stealth all over us—

but the spangled light never does get bold enough to brighten the river.

Against this the fighter jet flyover supposed to fire through the sky at noon
will shock the hell out of the kids.

It'll take days to talk the mock operations out of their minds.

All the while the clustered shrubs will let go their waves of wild tidings into the wind.

An amazing grace will ricochet off the current
the faithful keep going down into

and bewilder the high bluffs in repeat—

where the limbs of the ruined willows keep up their obscene their incessant their insurgent
weeping

in the air in the end in the perilous

ordinary glare—

Return Trip by Night

We coasted in idle down from the pass toward the white salt flats
that blazed up into a mind made entirely of light.

The wings of monarchs flared from the ditches in a storm of ill orange
that burned into the grillwork like jack tobacco curing to rot under the moon.

Low-slung rain reddened at dawn and made of the whole air a wild vow.

Hush. It was exactly *then*—

then that the puncture wounds we'd put for so long into wherever of ourselves was left
started to green at the edges, turn into history and heal.

The shaking eases up by late autumn, and then the pallor, as the blue asters open.

They are almost a sky.

There is a first full night of sleep.

Every so often the bored neighbors wing bottles into the alley.
The shattering against rock blows a shock of needles into the breeze.

Its noise is a fury—in the dark something fast, fleeing.

Accordingly

We've propped open the windows on sticks.
Heat sucks the cotton curtains in.

Dumb stunned noon,
out of which we drag two chairs to the shade of the cottonwoods
winter ripped up.

We hang our rags on the fence, careful not to bust the tiger lilies there.

In spite of every deadline we're up against, as if they had minds of their own,
our hands undo the buttons keeping these silly clothes on.

The blowback breaks with a sigh that rises like someone said
certain desires do.

Our knuckles are fat with salt from work and hardly bend,
though somehow this helps.

If it rains we'll go on in, or not.

In a while we'll dress the sores, drink and sleep and go at it again.

The washing hasn't been done in days.

The shadows tend.

Riptide

6.

We're talking now
in the ticking away of a few hot minutes on this lethal morning,
a Wednesday, September 28, two years into the war,

and there's dust on it—

all the time, on the entire place, there's no exception to the dust
all over the map northwest of Baghdad.

It might help to picture the recruiting station mobbed with citizens,
who, as they mill around and shift and squat in the hardpan yard,

seem to have no shadows in these diminishing moments
before the blast.

Imagine the suicide bomber.

Start with her face.

Not just what's public (eyes) as she approaches this place
but the features in secret, there behind her scarf,

and then her neck which is covered and her chest—
but where, look, the slightest disturbance of one stray wire
sprouts up in the folds,

then the shape of her draped waist where a thick belt's been packed
with ammo and metal balls and strapped on by her handlers
and cinched.

The trip switch is in easy reach.

She's fiddling with it every few seconds
like it needs to be fixed.

Like her hands need something on which to fix.

Like her hands need something to fix.

5.

The place was known as a civil operations center,
a complex of low-slung cinderblock where until a week before
our military processed damage claims—

to property, belongings, bodies, etc.—

but were now recruiting Iraqi men to turn into cops so they could
take over things.

There'd been a recent offensive in this town and news was
even the air still felt sore.

Tell me again who you are.

Tell me your reason for being here.

Your purpose your meaning tell me why this is a place for you to be.

She's making her way, she's got on the device,
she's in disguise, she's about to do an action that's not exactly

been done yet in this war by the someone she is—
the first female suicide bomber,

she is all of, what, maybe twenty (by the look of the shot of her severed head
someone running through the blowback smeared onto film and got aired live)

and at last in this heat of this very morning she's had enough of whatever it is

that finally compels a person like her, who will make the news,
to utter yes, consider me, I'll do it.

Because there's this itch in the mind.

    4.

There's this few minutes in the evening, in early autumn,
when my mouth still tastes like smoke, smoke and salad flowers,
and I go out for air.

It's the kind of weather that steals up your spine—
traces of dry lightning and the reek of iron under the grass—

and for a flash
it's one of those moments when you have no possessions.

Maybe like heaven might be if you believed heaven might be,
but then the ticking starts

and the wind kicks up and the itch in the mind
starts to go a bit frantic in the cantled thistle

and the motion of it rocks odor from the asters
and the shadow of that ripped willow doubles over,

lizards stir on the pocked clay that's suddenly stark in this light
and the cloud that's causing the limbs such confusion

presses down, like the feel of a hand along the small of the back.

When did these clothes get so frayed?
When did this gust of nettles get snagged on the hem of this day?

She's already thinking about how this day is going to go
(and it does).

As if she'd invented it.

_____

The offensive had gone something like this:

Sweeps all week
which in this war was our soldiers combing through crowds
and going in and out of houses, vehicles, twists of blind and dead-end alleys

asking who are you who is this what is your reason
(as if the checkpoints were already implicit)

and then, after the translation of whatever it is
we're talking about now gets lost in the backstory,

roundups, and convoys snaking in and out of the glare she's been squinting into
as they take the incorrect answers
away.

3.

In junk trucks, on foot, more loads arrive to interact with our forces
in the already evidentiary air that is still
very sore.

Which is after all a risk
under this sun—

insurgents being active as ever in this region

in which she got up this increasingly indescribable morning
and headed, in her condition, toward the succession of checkpoints

in a vehicle, got out, walked on as has been reported with the crowd
as if a part of some inevitable seasonal migration

through the next station and the next and so on.

This for hours.

After a while what should take longer gets hurried, for instance, the inquiries
at the final checkpoint,

and the exactitude with which even a versed soldier might pose them
turns in this disorienting air a bit scorched

and what's this about, what's this commotion all about
occurs, and whoever's at the moment a person of interest under questioning

simply gets motioned on
toward the cement service boxes hovering
over the dust-gorged heat

waves in the distance. Go ahead. Move on.

It's a small singe in the net through which she moves.

   2.

I'm not a person with another sort of fate.

Understand that it's not possible to come back from this war
very much alive. And so,

how to find a way into it—into the fray,
which with this itch of mine can't possibly stay shut to me.

I will be checked and be asked and be motioned through.
Will circulate and in this moving conduct myself as in drills.

Will as practiced put my body into recruitment.
And take it and plant it in the midst (will make a fate).

Like the bomb it is.

The something that's got to be done is an impending riptide
in the hot white air—

backward-arching particles,
the extremities closing in toward the rigid stem

and the motion of any insurrection that might still cling to the limbs
put down in a swift

mockery of hapless ash dusting the brick.

When did the horizon get so unstable,
as if to disregard us?

————————————

And so,
when she does cast down

the gaze of her very public eyes, and reaches her flexed palm to
yank the pin,

her kill-box will be a circular rippling-out in plastered blooms

from her waist like the blasted plumes of an ethereally lethal skirt,

a 360 staccato spray pattern of shrapnel that silvers
and sticks to the struck air

that is in the extension of this spectacular instant
so sick with pain

at just after 10:30 a.m. on this no longer random day,

and will have in its blood-slick grip eight humans about whom not much else

makes the news beyond their being in the way of this operation
mortally hurt, and, so,

thoroughly involved in dust.

Was the unrest ever more bewildering?
She did what?

Exactly.

   1.

What is it in the shadows of this understory
that drives the dessicated and now brittle leaves,

that hurries the dust into such mercenary dervishes—

I think it's not the wind we're talking about, given in at last to stupor,

and it's not exhaust off the vehicles that rush in the ruts,
to which the air has gotten used.

I've put white sheets on all the things to keep the granulations from settling
and shut each shade against the heat before going out.

It's not movement caused by breathing.

About this disturbance, I think, after thinking about it for days, it is
not even phenomenal,

and so, this morning, it was with the understanding that we are living now
in a target-rich environment

that I knelt down into the drought-singed garden

where the ripe unease of autumn reeks at high peak
and wasps mob the bruised fruit mash that lies on the dirt in spoils,

and any afterthoughts about what's still being called this conflict

run wild in their fervor through the escalation of upheaval

as do the bitterns flocked here, hovering over the dust,
as if it were time to go—

and in the air which this early in the season is still so far from still,
smoke tricks up from the hollow's fallow ground fires

and from my place in its wake I can see, as if this has never happened before,

the shriveled limbs of the heat-struck olive, which has no other fate
but to suffer the teasing of these merciless rainclouds

that trail their alluring promises all over the sky—

and then refuse to weep.

Occupational

But you were saying, I was saying—
together we stutter toward a stab at the everafter
and still this treaty between us shatters.

The swallow's leaf-rot nesting sours the breeze.
Aphids lace the startled iceplants with spit.

Even these cool midday shadows wouldn't correct our dreams
were we to sleep, and so the thinking, at this moment,
is of stalling whatever's next.

A momentous sight supernal is upon our countenance,
mutters the old man into his wine by the window.

By now whatever it might mean we believe.

Our children will perish one after another of the same greedy fever
and be buried along the way in the stinking weeds.

This much we know we know.
The roots will take the shape of another cradle by autumn.

The weather will be remembered for its epic aridity.

You will hold to a faith absurd in its forgiveness of God.
I will blind the eye of my beholder.

The Insurgency

I don't mean to go on about the stump.

Or talk anymore now about our vows, our wars, our frantic doing of something, anything.

There have been enough appointments canceled, and promises declined
on such short notice.

The workers arrived early with the machines, that's all.
Knock, knock.

———————————

No and no again to visitations, to any outings.
Weeks go by unaccounted and still undone after dark and the bodies fall.

Here goes the image that suggests inconsolability:
there is a tree in it, an elm.

The sky threatens to answer a prayer but then won't.

It is not exactly our own minds we go out of.

———————————

Hasn't this tree been our shelter, in service to this garden.

Someone swears *even if, even then*—it wasn't ready.

All winter the roots seemed to feed into a terminally dumb throb.

It hummed there, outside the window, in ways you'd never do anything about
in words. Something. Anything.

———————————

The team was on it at once, already sweating.
They brought it down in two hours: crown, canopy, trunk, felled.

I could go on, though just thinking makes the landscape hurt,
including the wild ivy that's lost its shade.

The glare upon the garden blinds—and there is nothing now
between us and that terrible sun.

Provisional Endings during Wartime

1.

I've been taking notes on the hive
for nine swarm seasons, and can report on their doings:

winter torpor lifts, flowers call, colony murmurs and swells,
scouts exit cells and flock to blooms, old queen stirs in her domain,

air warms, space gets tight, idea of quitting hive kicks in,
restlessness, tumult, wax and propolis get packed,

morning of the most dangerous day of their existence breaks,

regime in peril, authority denounced, leader obliges, multitude departs,
brave airlifting republic embarks on precarious dream.

Meanwhile,
everything but the bees seems to be getting even more bewildering.

2.

For instance, last week I got this letter from prisoner #178734:

"Awhile ago you wrote a story in the paper about the garbage house I grew up in. I was the oldest kid, and am now serving time in Lino Lakes prison but am innocent. Curious if you might write more about the way my life's going. There was lots of abuse, which isn't much of an excuse but, you know, possibly a reason."

The story—this was some time ago, on deadline—ran for pages, and went like this:

The first hint of what might be wrong was the stench of urine.

As the cops went in the place turned into a kind of funhouse, where the ground rises up and the walls shrink. Four feet high in piles was garbage—you name it, wrappers, rotted food, busted toys, appliances, ruined clothes, papers going back years.

*Inside were the nine-year-old boy, a baby in diapers perched on stacks of mashed trash,
and girl twins who were deaf, talking between themselves in rapid-fire sign by the fridge
roaches spilled from.*

*The girls slept on a mattress under piles of refuse matted by the weight of their bodies—to
get into bed they'd climb up and slide down a heap that was slick with human feces.*

"My mom and dad sort of just moved out," he told me at the time. *"The last years we
didn't have water, no heat, no lights, no electric, no phone. I'd go around the corner to the
Holiday station and steal food—bread mostly, and candy. I'd take the baby down there for a
bath. I tried to teach him to walk, too, but there was so much garbage he couldn't stand up
right."*

All four kids got carried out into the afternoon light, which made them squint as if it hurt.

   3.

I can only imagine an ending that begins
"Beside the jasmine in her halter top and snarled hair she clutches a pop bottle and laughs
and laughs, as the cease-fire holds,
as the silver fist of powder she's standing on
doesn't blow up, as if she could never be any more
beautiful."

   4.

Or, "Not in opposition to grief but in answer."

   5.

Anyway, here's a true story
my neighbor told me two weeks after getting home from the war:

I'm just off the night shift.
The moon's like busted glass on the sidewalk, and when I look up

my kitchen window's a gold print on the dark.

But, wait, what?—
I don't leave lights on, never do, so that little alarm
that's in my head now goes off.

I'm trained to wait things out so do, and then a shadow
crosses over, it's a body up there, a human one,

moved by the look of its movement by some kind of music going on,
and then another I don't know joins in,

and look, they're starting to sway, they're dancing, whoever they are, they are actually dancing,

they're a couple freaky kids necking in the groove, in the light of my own window,

one's shirtless with his head pitched back, one's hoisting her skirt, so I just let them,
and why not?—

I was just going to sleep it all off, everything, like every other night,

and figured hey it's not so cold out here, the sky's staining that faint pink,
here are these early sparrows, here's this decent breeze,

here's this strange music that isn't quite mine but that in their company
I now can hear.

6.

Mint farms.
Salt licks.
Shadows, even if orphaned.
Eclipses.
Litanies to do with mercy.
Stubbed toes full of quartz.
The Mohring Effect.
Perp walks.
Whatever's prelapsarian.
Lullabies.

Zambonis.
The hirsute of peppiness.
Dust that defies all organization.
Amulets.
Whims.

7.

Speaking of bees, one time I saw this swarm stuck to a traffic light.

The cluster gripped the mechanism like a fist, and lit up from the inside green then yellow
then red, for hours through the night.

People heard about it and drove down and circulated the block, stop and go
every time the bees switched color.

By midnight it was a motorcade, a carnival, a cruise ship, a freak bee incident,
it was phenomenal.

Hundreds, heretically, on impulse.

This in June, in Iowa, where I'm from, when it warms up and gets crowded,
when it's usually secrecy we'd all prefer.

Eventually a local beekeeper showed up with a brush and smoker to take the clump.
He whacked it with a pheromone stick over a box, and everyone booed.

We were by then all for the bees,

even when in their languorous, ponderous condition they rose up irked
and stung this handler.

And we shall be so rarefied in our souls that we shall go swiftly and whywhere,
says the anonymous author of a cloud I know,

is what I was thinking when, in apogee,
the swarm around daybreak climbed up the air and took wing.

Took wing. Who ever says that? It was a moment.

And did they.

All the way home I had the flavor of honey on my tongue,
which was the white clover crop, in bloom,

upwind.

  8.

Things fall apart. You mean to, but then you don't.
Or you do, but then you just lose track of it all.
For a while, perhaps, there was the desire. Later, a kind of fatigue.
Time gets away. Something slips—
a disconnect—
and the heat goes, the lights. Others, even the children, seem able to take care of
themselves.
Tomorrow you'll set all this chaos right.
But the thought gets lost underneath, in the undertow.
No one's watching anyway. No one's been notified.

"Somebody called it chaos—maybe that was you, in the story. At the time I thought it
was normal."

  9.

(notes from second cease-fire, interview #12)

mad wind and sky in a blown white dress

then a quick itch of heat up my spine like the sunlight's acid

stride's off-kilter as if chiseled from quartz

at last even birds emerged

ticking started up then like climbing back down a ladder

a little fire-heap

whoever couldn't get up straight knelt or just stayed flat

all the apparatus quivered

it was as if something like a spirit went around murmuring in every ear

one of us wound the clock

after some trouble the windows opened

nothing but molded roots we boiled them in snow we fed each other

　　10.

The door seems close enough to reach before the blast—

　　11.

And finally, this:
the last day I did temp work I left my beige cube at break-time to join with likewise temps
in beige hose by the elevator, and ding—

it opens and out blasts this

utmost salutation of insanely warm wild lilac-laced purple late-spring air
hauled up off earth

and into the highrise, where I get in　　and go down　　and go out.

　　12.

Around 3 A.M., as if nothing were ever final,
all the potholes in the buckled tar iced back over

and across one a little dog, a black toy mix something,
started to skate in oblong arcs on all fours.

The power was out so the only light on this animal was from the last fires,
which lent it an almost holy glow as it glided—

and I must say the orbit this mutt achieved, in relation to outer space,

etching its own trajectory of elegant elliptical ease across the ice,

no unbalanced force around
to interrupt its dedication to constancy in direction and speed,

without faltering, sure in its undulating allegiance to the laws of universal motion,

made this animal, this earthling, for this moment, our planet's most devoted citizen.

13.

Everything getting more bewildering, such as:

we never got around to chopping down that oak that's been sick
since before the kid who's swinging crazylike from it now on a tire was born.

The cheerleader who just broke her neck falling off a human pyramid gets hauled away
on a gurney, still semaphoring her arms and screaming *Go team.*

The children play keep-away all the way into dusk, the noise of the river in their throats,
fierce, undaunted, as if none of them will ever be suspects.

The beater junker you bought off the arson unit ages ago hasn't broken down once,
even on our honeymoon.

The mob with its torches comes this close to a riot,
then shifts, with the wind, and doesn't.

Every time I'm near this river,
I have the dream of stripping down and just cannonballing in and maybe I'm crazy but
lately it seems to be getting more urgent.

—Oh, and don't forget about being law-abiding.

Don't forget what it might mean, at any moment, on any given day,
to be law-abiding.

14.

The boy was nine years old.

Nine.

In answer to your inquiry: yes, I will.

15.

One of us notices the azure stars of flax at noon and tells the other, who later remembers
the azure stars of flax at noon and tells the other, who'd forgotten.

16.

Yes. And—

Acknowledgments

I'm indebted to the editors of several journals for first publishing these poems, at various stages in their evolution:

American Literary Review (poetry editors: Bruce Bond and Corey Marks): Sections from
    "One Summer under Occupation Reports Its News & Weather"
Fuori (editor: Sarah Fox): Some language in these poems first appeared in *Edition 1:1*
Lush and *Spout* (editor: John Colburn): Sections from "One Summer under Occupation
    Reports Its News & Weather" and "Blowback"
Nimrod (editor: Francine Ringold): "Riptide" and "Kill-Box"
Post Road (poetry editor: Mark Conway): "The Insurgency"
Swerve (editor: Fred Schmalz): "Highrise," sections from "One Summer under Occupation
    Reports Its News & Weather," "Doorway, with Citizen," "Requiescat," "Wind Camp,"
    and "Occupational"

My gratitude extends to the Minnesota State Arts Board, Can Serrat International Art Center (El Bruc, Catalonia, Spain), and Jerome Foundation, whose staff, funding, and high purposes assisted me in putting this book together.

Printmaker Fred Hagstrom and I collaborated on an artist's book that illustrates the text of "Kill-Box." I thank him for suggesting it in the first place, and for constructing the book and its fine black box.

Joanna Rawson is the author of a previous poetry collection, *Quarry*. Her work has appeared in *American Poetry Review, Antioch Review, Mother Jones, Nimrod,* and *Salon.* She has received awards from the Association of Writers & Writing Programs and the Society of Professional Journalists. She writes for *Public Art Review, Utne* magazine, and other periodicals, and works as a Master Gardener in Northfield, Minnesota, where she lives with her husband and their two girls.

This book was designed by Rachel Holscher. It is set in Times type by BookMobile Design and Publishing Services, and manufactured by Versa Press on acid-free paper.